31 Days to Living as a New Believer

Also by R. Larry Moyer

31 Days to Contagious Living: A Daily Devotional Guide on Modeling Christ to Others

31 Days with the Master Fisherman: A Daily Devotional on Bringing Christ to Others

Dear God, I'm Ticked Off: Answering the Spiritual Complaints and Concerns of Others

Free and Clear: Understanding and Communicating God's Offer of Eternal Life

Growing in the Family: 8 Vital Relationships for the Growing Christian

Larry Moyer's How-To Book on Personal Evangelism

Welcome to the Family! Understanding Your New Relationship to God and Others
(By EvanTell Resources)

31 Days to Living as a New Believer

R. LARRY MOYER

kregel
PUBLICATIONS

Grand Rapids, MI 49501

31 Days to Living as a New Believer

© 2002 by R. Larry Moyer

Published by Kregel Publications, a division of Kregel, Inc., P.O. Box 2607, Grand Rapids, MI 49501. For more information about Kregel Publications, visit our Web site: www.kregel.com.

Unless otherwise noted, Scripture quotations are from the New King James Version. Copyright © 1979, 1980, 1982, Thomas Nelson, Inc., Publishers.

Cover design: John M. Lucas

Library of Congress Cataloging-in-Publication Data
Moyer, R. Larry (Richard Larry)
    31 days to living as a new believer / by R. Larry Moyer.
        p.   cm.
    1. New church members—Prayer-books and devotions—English. 2. I. Title: Thirty-one days to living as a new believer. II. Title.
BV4596.N48 M69   2002   242—dc21   2002016085
                                                                CIP

ISBN 0-8254-3172-7

Printed in the United States of America

1 2 3 4 5 / 06 05 04 03 02

*To the memory of Bill Rodenberg,
one of EvanTell's certified
You Can Tell It! instructors.
The consuming passion of his life
was to introduce lost people
to Jesus Christ.*

Preface: Wait a Minute!

(Don't charge ahead until you read this first.)

CONGRATULATIONS! Having become a Christian, you have begun first-class living.

Why? Is this because there'll be no more problems, heartaches, or suffering? No, there'll be plenty of all of those.

What makes the Christian life first-class is two-fold. For one, you *know* that when you die you'll be in the presence of the King of Kings, Jesus Christ—forever. Nothing can change that. John 5:24 promises, "Most assuredly, I say to you, he who hears My word and believes in Him who sent Me has everlasting life, and shall not come into judgment, but has passed from death into life." Your eternal life is guaranteed because you accepted what Jesus Christ did for you on the cross. He died as your substitute and then rose from the dead. Having trusted Christ, you have eternal life—not because of what you've done for Him but because of what Christ did for you.

Second, you've just met the One who wants to

become your best and dearest friend. Jesus Christ is not merely with you, He is living *within* you. Paul the apostle, one of the men God used to write the Bible, spoke of Christ as living within: "I have been crucified with Christ; it is no longer I who live, but Christ lives in me; and the life which I now live in the flesh I live by faith in the Son of God, who loved me and gave Himself for me" (Galatians 2:20). He is your friend, and He wants to help you with everything you face in life—bar nothing. That's why you'll want to know Him better.

And that's where I want to help. I want to help you get to know Him better. I've called this devotional *31 Days to Living as a New Believer* because it contains thirty-one truths, truths that I wish someone had told me when I first came to Christ. Not only would I have been helped tremendously in adjusting to my new life in Christ, I would have started growing faster. We'll talk about everything, from temptation to do wrong, to our struggles even when we're doing right. We'll talk about things related to your family at home and to your family at church. You'll discover that it's exciting to know Him, and it's exciting to walk with Him one day at a time.

Ready? You're about to eat at the buffet of the Word of God, digesting truths that make you a spiritually strong Christian.

Your brother in God's forever family,
R. Larry Moyer

*Your new life is about
relationship, not religion.*

To Read

> *Come to Me, all you who labor and are heavy
> laden, and I will give you rest. Take My yoke upon
> you and learn from Me, for I am gentle and lowly
> in heart, and you will find rest for your souls. For
> My yoke is easy and My burden is light.*
> —Matthew 11:28–30

To Consider

For me, religion always came up short. Sometimes I found it confusing and frustrating. I felt I could never be good enough for God to accept me, and I was never sure how good I had to be in order to be good enough. I misunderstood, though, the vast difference between religion and Christ.

In the above verses, Jesus Christ invited those who "labor and are heavy laden" to come to Him. The two major religious factions of Christ's day laid down an enormous amount of regulations to follow in order to be accepted by God. The religious leaders insisted upon enforcing an endless list of dos and don'ts. One of those regulations even stipulated certain days on which you couldn't hit a donkey with your whip! You can imagine how confusing, tiring, and frustrating those regulations were.

Christ was passionate that we understand how different His instructions are. The word *yoke* refers to a wooden frame placed upon the shoulders that makes a burden easier to bear. In the verses above *yoke* refers to Christ's instructions on how to live a life pleasing to God. Why is His yoke so different?

First, you've been saved through your personal faith in Christ, so you're not living for Him in order to be accepted by God. You're living for Him because you've already been accepted. Second, you're living for someone who is "gentle and lowly in heart"—humble, not haughty. That kind of person is easy to follow. Third, while He is teaching you how to live, He's right there giving you strength. That's why He exclaimed, "My yoke is easy. My burden is light."

If you do wrong, He's sympathetic and understanding, forgiving you and helping you to be stronger next time. Living for Him becomes a delight, not a duty, because living for Him is centered on a relationship, not regulations. Religion can be burdensome. A relationship with Christ is a relief.

To Illustrate

A book called *Mushrooms on the Moor* contains the story of a believer who knew that at the center of the Christian life was a relationship with the One who had died for him. Eventually, the believer became ill and was confined to bed. A document was brought to him that required his signature. He took a pen and held it for a long moment, signed the document, then fell back upon his pillow, dead. It then became obvious how grateful that believer was for the Savior and how privileged he felt to live for Him. On the paper the believer had written not his own name but the name *Jesus*—the One he was about to see face to face.

To Meditate

Religion focuses on the regulations you must follow to be accepted by God. The Christian life focuses on your relationship with God, a relationship made possible because, through Christ, He has accepted you.

To Pray

Take a moment to praise God for bringing you into an eternal relationship with the Savior. Give Him thanks that you can now live for Him out of gratitude and delight.

Day 2

Pray! Pray! Pray! Pray! Pray!

To Read

Pray without ceasing.

—1 Thessalonians 5:17

To Consider

Consider what you've learned about Jesus Christ so far. If you had spent three years with Him, as His twelve disciples did, what would you have wanted Him to teach you?

Do you know what they requested? They said, "Lord, teach us to pray" (Luke 11:1). They were apparently struck that He was a person given to prayer.

As we walk in His footsteps and become Christlike we, too, need to pray. The more we pray, the more we come to depend completely upon the Lord. In the apostle Paul's closing of his letter to the Thessalonians, he mentions many things vital to their spiritual well-being. He included everything from not returning evil for evil to having a grateful heart.

In the midst of those injunctions he said three words powerful in meaning: "Pray without ceasing."

Does that mean a person *never* stops praying? In one sense no, and in another sense yes. Nobody is able to talk to God twenty-four hours a day. But Paul's point is that an attitude of prayer is something that should consistently characterize our lives. There should never be a day we do not pray, and some days we should find ourselves praying many times. Prayer becomes as natural as breathing. As someone once said, "Prayer should come from your lips as water comes from a dripping faucet." Pray when you get up, and pray an hour after you're up. Pray on your way to work, and pray on your way home.

What if you don't have the time to pray? Prayer is not a matter of having time but of taking time, of knowing how important prayer is. What if you don't know how to express what you feel? Don't worry about that. Just talk to God the way you'd talk to a friend.

To Illustrate

Years ago I had the privilege of leading a woman to Christ. She was recently divorced and the mother of a young child. As we talked about spiritual growth, I stressed the need for prayer. Her comment was, "I don't know how to pray." I responded, "Just talk to God the way you would to a friend. Why don't we start right now? Just talk." She bowed her head and said, "Dear God, this is Clara. It's been a while since you've heard from me but we're going to be talking a lot more in the coming weeks." I've never heard a prayer more meaningful or sincere. Praying became a regular part of her day and caused her to grow spiritually.

To Meditate

The Person who saved you should hear from you the most, and talking to Him is talking to the One nearest you.

To Pray

Ask God to make prayer one of the most prominent parts of your Christian walk. Ask Him to give you a desire to pray and for persistence in prayer.

Day 3

Don't talk to God about a few things. Talk to Him about everything.

To Read

> *Be anxious for nothing, but in everything by prayer and supplication, with thanksgiving, let your requests be made known to God; and the peace of God, which surpasses all understanding, will guard your hearts and minds through Christ Jesus.*
> —Philippians 4:6–7

To Consider

Not everyone is easy to talk to. Some people are always in a rush; whatever you have to say, you'd better say it fast. And sometimes what you want to say is of such a private nature, it's hard to talk at all.

But that's what is exciting about your newfound friend, Jesus Christ. He wants to hear from you, and anything that matters to you matters to Him even more.

What do the above verses tell you to worry about?

The answer is *nothing!* What's the alternative? Paul the apostle explained to the Philippians, "But in everything by prayer and supplication, with thanksgiving, let your requests be made known to God." The word *prayer* relates to an attitude of complete dependence upon Him. The word *supplication* refers to your specific requests. These requests may concern spiritual needs such as the need to forgive others, or physical needs such as health and finances.

But notice that other important word—*everything*. When God says something, He means what He says. He says *everything* because He means *everything*. Burdened about a relative who is dying of cancer? Talk to God about it. Concerned about how impatient you are at times? Talk to Him about it. Afraid that your income won't be sufficient to meet unexpected bills this month? Take it to Him in prayer.

What will happen as you do? Paul explained: "And the peace of God, which surpasses all understanding, will guard your hearts and minds through Christ Jesus." *Guard* is a military term, depicting a Roman soldier who keeps guard before the palace and protects all those inside. God is saying, then, that if you take your concerns to Him in prayer and leave them there, a peace beyond description will guard your heart and mind. He'll keep you from a panic attack, anxiety, or even a mental breakdown.

To Illustrate

Tom, a believer, sat up late in his study worrying about many things. Undoubtedly, the same concerns came to his mind that come to ours—finances, health, the future, relationships. Finally, Tom felt as though the Lord was standing in front of him saying, "Son, you go to bed. I'll sit up the rest of the night." Tom then realized that God wanted him to give those burdens to Him. Tom gave those concerns to God, left them there, and enjoyed a good night's sleep.

To Meditate

A comfort in being a Christian is that we only have to worry about the things that God cannot handle!

To Pray

Think of three items that presently cause you the greatest anxiety. Right now, talk to God about those three things. Each time they come to your mind, remind yourself to place those concerns on His shoulders, not on yours.

Day 4

You can bring Christ to your friends, but God has to bring your friends to Christ.

To Read

> *No one can come to Me unless the Father who sent Me draws him; and I will raise him up at the last day.*
>
> —John 6:44

To Consider

Now that you're a Christian, you probably want to introduce Christ to the whole world, and *especially* to those who are closest to you.

But speaking about Christ to others, whether friends or strangers, can be frustrating. They may not sense the need for Christ the way you did. At times you'll probably feel like throwing your hands up and saying, "How do I reach them?"

Be careful not to take on God's responsibility. God wants you to bring Christ to others—to anybody, anywhere. But God brings them or "draws" them to Christ. Christ's words allowed for no exceptions: "*No one* can come to Me *unless* the Father who sent Me *draws* him."

Think about your own conversion. You may have been spiritually rebellious, or maybe you were religious but didn't understand that eternal life was a free gift. Regardless, you would have never seen your need for Christ if He, through the Holy Spirit, had not started to work in your life. The Holy Spirit may have used a friend, a sermon, a pamphlet, a book, or just those quiet moments when you were reflecting upon life—or more particularly, *your* life. But *God* brought you to Christ. Others could only bring Christ to you.

The same goes for those whom you want to know Him. So ask God to give you an opportunity to present the gospel clearly to them. Then pray, asking God to show them their need and to bring them to the Savior. (If you're not sure how to present the gospel, write to us here at EvanTell. We'll send you a free copy of our *"May I Ask You a Question?"* booklet, which will guide you in reaching others.)

To Illustrate

In 1998 I was speaking in Sequim, Washington. A sixty-eight-year-old man approached me and said, "I want to thank you for being instrumental in my salvation." He then explained, "Back in 1980 you spoke at a church in Ohio. I came each night but did not respond to your invitation to trust Christ. You were so burdened for my salvation that you stopped by my house on the way to the airport to talk with me some more. I still resisted. What you never knew was that I trusted Christ before you even got to the airport." Try as I might, ultimately it was God who had to bring that man to Christ. I could only bring Christ to him.

To Meditate

In terms of reaching others for Christ, you can do the conversing. God has to do the converting.

To Pray

Think of a person you would like to see come to Christ. Ask God to give you the opportunity to speak to that person this week. As you do so, ask God to help that person understand and acknowledge his or her need of the Savior.

Day 5

Let Jesus Christ be number one in your life.

To Read

According to my earnest expectation and hope that in nothing I shall be ashamed, but with all boldness, as always, so now also Christ will be magnified in my body, whether by life or by death. For to me, to live is Christ, and to die is gain.
—Philippians 1:20–21

To Consider

Before you became a believer, what was number one in your life? Was it family, friends, money, fame, recognition, success, a job, a house, a motorcycle, a car? Those things in their proper place are fine, but now God has given to you something bigger and better as a *major* focus.

Paul the apostle declared, "For to me, to live is Christ, and to die is gain." Paul resolved that at the center of his life would be one Person—Jesus Christ. Everything Paul said and everything he did was examined through his relationship with the Savior—

the Person he most wanted to please. *Nobody* and *nothing* had greater control in Paul's life than Christ.

What made that so rewarding? When Paul died, he would have no regrets. Since he had received God's free gift of eternal life, he would be in Christ's presence forever. He would have even more of Christ than he had on earth. At the moment of Paul's death, any loss he suffered would be merely what was not number one in his life.

Consider Paul's attitude this way. If we complete the thought, "For to me, to live is _____" with any response other than Christ, we ultimately experience loss instead of gain. If, for example, we say, "For me, to live is money," then to die is loss because we can't take money with us. If we say, "For me, to live is my status at work," then to die is loss because we leave our jobs behind. If we say, "For me, to live is friends," then to die is loss because friends will remain on earth while we go to heaven. Only when we live for Christ and keep Him number one in our lives does death become gain instead of loss. And as we enter heaven we will have even more of the Person who was our number one on earth.

To Illustrate

Anglican war hero Herbert Cragg once received a letter from a very mature Christian. The postscript to that letter had a tremendous impact on his life:

"To many people, Jesus is nothing at all. To some people, Jesus is something. But to too few people, Jesus is everything." Don't make Jesus Christ something. Make Him *everything* in your life. Keep Him in first place.

To Meditate

In terms of what has eternal value, always remember that Jesus Christ can take the place of anything, but nothing can take the place of Christ.

To Pray

Ask God on a weekly basis to help you examine your priorities. Ask Him to help you keep Christ first, above everyone and everything in your life.

Day 6

Proper priorities are essential to spiritual growth.

To Read

> *If then you were raised with Christ, seek those things which are above, where Christ is, sitting at the right hand of God. Set your mind on things above, not on things on the earth.*
>
> —Colossians 3:1–2

To Consider

Sooner or later everybody has to prioritize. It doesn't matter if you're running a household of four or managing a corporation of four hundred. Prioritizing is also important to your growth as a Christian.

Now that you belong to Christ, the same power that raised Christ from the grave is yours as well. You have been "raised with Christ." As we examined yesterday, Jesus Christ needs to be your number one priority. With Him as your first priority, though, where does that leave everything else in your life?

Because Jesus Christ, in all His resurrection power, lives inside of you, you have the ability to live on a higher plane. You are personally related to the One who sits at the right hand of God. Your new position and relationship allow you to live as you could not otherwise live.

What does life on a higher plane mean? The answer is found in two almost identical phrases. Scripture says, "Seek those things which are above," and "Set your mind on things above." The things that matter most to Christ should matter most to you. Things that are eternal are more important than things that are temporal. Spiritual things are more important than material things. Things of the heavenly realm are more important than things of the earthly realm.

Does that mean we neglect our families or are irresponsible on our jobs? Definitely not. Nor does it mean that we can not enjoy the comfort of a new home or a ride in our new car. God wants us to appreciate and enjoy those comforts. At issue is where we put our emphasis and what we treat as the *most* important. Being godly is more important than being popular. Interaction with a neighbor in need of our friendship is more essential than catching a TV program. Our study of Scriptures is more critical than our study of the stock market. Talking to God in prayer is more important than time spent on the telephone.

What is high on Christ's list of priorities should be high on ours. What is low on His list should be low on ours. Growing as a Christian involves thinking and doing things in order of importance.

To Illustrate

In 1851, the renowned Swedish opera singer Jenny Lind went to New York City at the height of her fame in the musical world. While visiting a church service she was introduced to Christ and trusted Him as Savior. Much to the dismay of her fans, the theater became less important to her as she pursued heavenly goals. Later, when asked why she eventually abandoned the stage, she responded, "With each passing day, show business made me think less of my Bible and hardly anything at all of what lies beyond life. So what else could I do?"

To Meditate

As we prioritize properly, the things of heaven should move up on our list. The things of earth should move down.

To Pray

Examine carefully that which is most important in your life. If something is not prioritized properly, ask God to help you put it in its proper place. Then ask Him to help you week by week to maintain those proper priorities.

Day 7

Salvation is the one gift you can never lose!

To Read

And I give them eternal life, and they shall never perish; neither shall anyone snatch them out of My hand. My Father, who has given them to Me, is greater than all; and no one is able to snatch them out of My Father's hand.

—John 10:28–29

To Consider

I found two things very exciting when I first came to Christ. These two things still excite me. One was receiving absolutely free His gift of eternal life. The other was *never* being able to lose it.

That's right—never. In the gospel of John, Jesus referred to Christians as His sheep. Using the strongest language possible, He said, "I give them eternal life, and they shall *never* perish; neither shall anyone snatch them out of My hand." Christ used the unusual word *snatch* because His imagery was that of a wolf, dragging a sheep away from the fold. His point was that nothing we do, and nothing our enemy Satan does, can ever remove us from Him.

How is this possible? Because in order to lose our salvation in Christ, it would take a force greater than God Himself. Jesus continued, "My Father, who has given them to Me, is greater than all; and no one is able to snatch them out of My Father's hand." We are forever a part of God's family, not because of how strong we are as sheep but because of who the Shepherd is. Our heavenly Father is all powerful and keeps us forever secure in Christ.

As Christians we may stumble or fall into sin. God wants us to confess that sin to Him. But He never takes back His free gift. Satan will attack us in numerous ways. He may even try to get us to be disobedient to the Savior. But when we turn away from God, He never turns away from us.

That's what you call love! That's what you call security! *We* are not holding *Him*. We are secure in Christ because *He* is holding *us*.

To Illustrate

A mountain climber in the Alps came to a dangerous point in his ascent. The only way he could continue was to place his foot in the outstretched hands of the guide, who had anchored himself a little way ahead of him. The man paused for a moment. He looked below to the spot where he would fall to his death if anything went wrong. The guide noticed his hesitation and then said, "Have no fear. In all my years of service, my hands have never yet lost a single person!" We are safe now, and we are safe forever, in the hands of Jesus our Savior.

To Meditate

The exciting thing about coming to Christ is that the one gift we needed most is the one gift we can never lose.

To Pray

Praise God for two things—that He brought you to Him and gave you eternal life, and that He will never take back His gift. Praising God for your *eternal* salvation should be a regular part of your life.

Day 8

What you get out of church is a great reason for going in.

To Read

And let us consider one another in order to stir up love and good works, not forsaking the assembling of ourselves together, as is the manner of some, but exhorting one another, and so much the more as you see the Day approaching.

—Hebrews 10:24–25

To Consider

Think of when you last participated on a sports team, whether it was a Little League baseball team or a bowling league. When you hit a home run or bowled a strike, the whole team cheered. If you won the game, you all won together; if you lost the game, you all lost together. You experienced the ups and downs together as a team, one unit.

The same thing happens when believers come together within a local church. The writer of Hebrews was concerned that some believers were discarding the need to be with each other. He encouraged them not to forsake, or abandon, their time together. But why is assembling as believers important?

The reason Paul gives is both positive and productive. It's the way we "consider one another in order to stir up love and good works." God never meant the Christian life to be lived alone. When we come together as believers, we have a common Savior in Jesus Christ. But we also have common experiences. Perhaps we are discouraged because we have a non-Christian relative who misrepresents us to the family. Maybe we still have things to deal with because of past sins. We may be struggling with a health problem or a difficulty at work.

By coming together in the local church we can express mutual concern and encouragement. We can pray with each other and for each other. We can sing praise together to help us focus on the awesomeness of God. We can study Scripture together and gain from one another's insights and observations.

Our encouragement of one another should only increase as we look forward to the second coming of Christ, what the writer of Hebrews calls "the Day approaching." Knowing He could return at any moment, we should be more eager than ever to come together and encourage one another to remain faithful to Christ.

Through involvement in a local church, you can

be strengthened and be used by God to strengthen others.

To Illustrate

A driver traveling from Alberta to the Yukon did not know a four-wheel drive was needed through a particular pass in the mountains. At breakfast prior to the journey, two truckers warned, "This passage is dangerous in weather like this." Nevertheless, the driver insisted, "I'm determined to try." One trucker responded, "Well, then I guess we'll just have to hug you." He went on to explain, "We'll put one truck in front of you and one in the rear—the front truck will break a trail and warn of any dangers ahead, and the rear truck will be behind to help if you should get into trouble. We'll get you through the mountains." They did, and the driver safely made it through the pass. In this pass called life, our involvement in a local church is one way we "hug" and encourage each other.

To Meditate

The church is a place where we can walk in discouraged and walk out encouraged.

To Pray

Ask God to help you find a church that teaches a portion of Scripture each Sunday. Then attend there regularly, and ask Him to surround you with people with whom you can practice mutual encouragement.

Day 9

Temptations will come, but God always gives you a way out.

To Read

No temptation has overtaken you except such as is common to man; but God is faithful, who will not allow you to be tempted beyond what you are able, but with the temptation will also make the way of escape, that you may be able to bear it.

—1 Corinthians 10:13

To Consider

When you came to Christ, Satan lost! He wanted you as part of his kingdom—an eternal hell. Through Christ, you are so certain of entering heaven, it's as if you're already there.

Since Satan cannot change your eternal destiny, he will try to keep you from impacting others for Christ through your life and witness. He will do that through temptation, enticing you to do wrong. He'll always use your weakest area, whether it has been immorality, drug addiction, pride, or gossip. Don't be surprised by this; *expect* temptation.

Paul the apostle addressed the Christians in Corinth, who also faced temptations. He told them three things that apply today as well. First, the temptations we face are those that any believer faces. They are temptations that are common to man. There is nothing spiritually wrong with us because we are being tempted.

The second thing Paul tells us is that God will never let us be tempted beyond what we are able to bear. God knows our breaking points, and He—not Satan—is in control. So if we give in to temptation we cannot excuse ourselves by saying, "I just couldn't take it anymore." Had the temptation been more than we could take, God would not have allowed it.

The third thing Paul tells us in 1 Corinthians 10:13 is how God helps us to experience victory over each temptation. He *always* provides a way of escape. If the temptation relates to pornography, we can avoid the bookstore we once frequented. If the temptation relates to uncontrolled anger, we can avoid speaking or doing anything until those feelings subside. But God will *always* provide a way to escape temptation.

Do everything you can to avoid situations in which you are tempted—but when tempted, look for a way to escape. It's there!

To Illustrate

After the French Revolution, the son of Louis XVI of France was turned over to vicious men who subjected him to the worst possible influences. They desired that he disgrace his name and position and make a mockery of the royal court. In the face of all temptations, the prince replied, "I cannot do that for I am the son of a king." When tempted to do wrong, remember you are a child of *the* King. Choose His escape, not Satan's temptation.

To Meditate

When temptation strikes, God's responsibility is to provide the way of escape; your responsibility is to take it.

To Pray

Ask God to help you be alert to areas of your life in which you are especially vulnerable to temptation. Then be obedient in saying yes to the way of escape and no to the way of temptation.

Day 10

God presents to you an exciting opportunity. It's called discipleship.

To Read

When He had called the people to Himself, with His disciples also, He said to them, "Whoever desires to come after Me, let him deny himself and take up his cross, and follow Me."

—Mark 8:34

To Consider

As you grow spiritually, you'll want to *invest* your life, not just go through the activities involved in living it. You'll want to know that your life counts for something that matters to God.

That's why God invites you to be a disciple. The word *disciple* means "learner." A growing disciple is a person who, having trusted Christ, is following after Him and is completely surrendered to whatever God wants to do with the disciple's life. God uses some disciples in secular vocations and others in Christian ministry.

One caution! Whereas our eternal salvation is a free gift, discipleship involves a cost. Observe the phrases God uses to explain what discipleship is and the cost it involves.

Let him deny himself. We must be willing to give up the ownership, or control, of our lives. Instead of asking, "What do *I* want to do with my life?" we must ask, "What does *God* want to do with my life?" Instead of directing God, you must be willing to let Him direct you.

Take up his cross. The cross represented humiliation and the method by which the worst criminals were crucified. *Taking up the cross* refers to the ridicule and persecution we sometimes suffer when we take a stand for the Savior. Some have even suffered physical death because of their commitment to Christ.

Follow Me. God wants us to daily learn from Him what constitutes godly living and then respond in obedience. His instructions may be in the area of parenting or prayer. He wants us to learn *how* to live the life that honors Him, and then go live it.

Although discipleship involves a cost, it is well worth it. Your life counts for something eternal because He directs and uses you. Better than anyone, God knows how your life can count.

To Illustrate

In his book *Priority One,* Norm Lewis relates that somebody asked Emily Post, the noted authority on manners, what to do if an invitation to the White House conflicted with a previous engagement. She answered, "An invitation to the White House is a summons which takes precedent over any previous engagement." An invitation to discipleship has such priority that it ought not be declined.

To Meditate

In light of the cost that Christ paid so that we could become Christians, no cost is too great that we might be called His disciples.

To Pray

Think carefully through the costs of being a disciple. Then, if you are prepared to do so, tell God in prayer, "I'm surrendering myself to You as Your disciple. Use me as You please."

You cannot live the Christian life. It's impossible.

To Read

*I have been crucified with Christ; it is no longer I
who live, but Christ lives in me; and the life which
I now live in the flesh I live by faith in the Son of
God, who loved me and gave Himself for me.*
——Galatians 2:20

To Consider

God has not called you to an easy life. He has called
you to an *impossible* life. In and of yourself, you cannot live the life God now wants you to live.

But the great news is that God doesn't expect you
to. Instead, He wants you to *let Him live through you.*

In the above verse, Paul spoke of two things, without which nobody can live for Christ. The first could
be called identification. When Paul said, "I have been
crucified with Christ," he didn't mean that he hung
on a cross alongside of Christ. Rather, he realized

that his good works would not make him acceptable to God. Instead, only through Jesus' substitutionary work on the cross could Paul stand completely righteous in God's eyes. Having trusted Christ, Paul knew that he was identified with Christ in His death and resurrection. Christ was living spiritually in Paul. Paul no longer had to be controlled by sin, but could live in the power that brought the Savior up from the grave.

The second thing we need in order to live for Christ is dependence. Paul continued, "And the life which I now live in the flesh I live by faith in the Son of God, who loved me and gave Himself for me." Paul knew that only through Christ's power could he love, forgive, practice self-control, have a consistent prayer life, and be a positive witness, plus everything else that is part of a God-honoring life.

You cannot approach the Christian life saying, "I can do this." Instead, you must approach it saying, "God, with your help I can do this." Your identification with Christ sets you free from the control of sin. Your dependence upon Christ helps you live a life you could not otherwise live.

To Illustrate

On June 12, 1979, a twenty-six-year-old man made aviation history. He flew a pedal-powered plane across the English Channel. As he took off from England and flew for three hours, he was rarely more than fifteen feet above the water. Finally, after covering twenty-two miles, he landed exhausted on a beach in France. For a short distance such a feat was possible. Human-powered flying is not, however, a practical form of transportation. No human can sustain the necessary energy to complete long and repeated flights. Similarly, we cannot live the Christian life pedaling on our own power. Instead, we must depend upon Christ to live His life through us.

To Meditate

God asks you to depend upon Christ to live a life so supernatural that only He can live it.

To Pray

Confess to Christ that you cannot live the life He wants you to live. Ask Him to keep you ever conscious that He lives inside of you, and that you must daily depend upon Him to live His life through you.

Day 12

Keep your eyes upon Christ, not upon Christians.

To Read

Therefore we also, since we are surrounded by so great a cloud of witnesses, let us lay aside every weight, and the sin which so easily ensnares us, and let us run with endurance the race that is set before us, looking unto Jesus, the author and finisher of our faith, who for the joy that was set before Him endured the cross, despising the shame, and has sat down at the right hand of the throne of God.

—Hebrews 12:1–2

To Consider

Any conscientious Christian wants to live a life that encourages others. But don't be naive; Christians *do* fail. That's why, lest we be disappointed, it's important to keep our eyes upon Christ, not upon Christians.

Hebrews 11 lists men and women of faith, the ones referred to as "so great a cloud of witnesses." They trusted God to do the impossible. Nevertheless, upon whom did the writer of Hebrews tell his readers to focus their eyes?

As admirable as were the Old Testament figures the writer mentioned, the One he told them to focus their eyes upon was Jesus, "the author and finisher of our faith." As the *author*, He has gone ahead of us, blazing a trail so to speak, and has brought us to Him, has given us His free gift of eternal life, and has laid out the path for us to follow. As the *finisher*, He reached the end of that task successfully. After enduring the cross and its awful shame, He took His exalted position at the right hand of the throne of God.

What a model, what a leader, to focus our eyes upon. Many Christians will encourage us, but at times those same Christians may disappoint us. As we follow Christ's example, He will never disappoint us, and we will have no regrets. When we join Him in heaven we, too, will share in the victory He has experienced.

To Illustrate

The story is told of Cyrus, the founder of the Persian Empire, who captured a prince and his family. He asked the prisoner, "What will you give me if I release you?" The prince replied, "Half of my wealth." Cyrus then asked, "And if I release your children?" The prince responded, "Everything I possess." Cyrus continued, "And if I release your wife?" The prince responded, "I will give myself." Cyrus was so moved with the prisoner's devotion that he freed them all. As the family returned home, the prince asked his wife, "Wasn't Cyrus a handsome man?" With love for her husband reflected in her eyes, she responded, "I didn't notice. I could only keep my eyes upon you—the one who was willing to give himself for me."

To Meditate

As believers, our primary focus must always be upon Christ, not upon Christians.

To Pray

Ask God to keep your eyes focused upon Jesus Christ. Then ask Him to help you look at the Christian life as if it were a race and, with patience and discipline, to daily live the life He wants you to live.

Day 13

Be encouraged—but never satisfied—by where you are spiritually.

To Read

> *Not that I have already attained, or am already perfected; but I press on, that I may lay hold of that for which Christ Jesus has also laid hold of me. Brethren, I do not count myself to have appre-hended; but one thing I do, forgetting those things which are behind and reaching forward to those things which are ahead, I press toward the goal for the prize of the upward call of God in Christ Jesus.*
> —Philippians 3:12–14

To Consider

Discontentment can destroy us. If we're not sat-isfied with our incomes, we could become greedy and materialistic. If we're not satisfied with the way we look, we could become self-focused and vain. If we're not satisfied with our mates, we could become immoral and fall into adultery.

In one area, however, discontentment can be used to our advantage to stimulate spiritual growth. Be encouraged—but never satisfied—by where you are spiritually.

Consider Paul. Although his knowledge of Christ grew deeper and deeper, Paul felt he never knew Him well enough. By "forgetting those things which are behind," Paul likely was not thinking of past failures and mistakes for which he had been forgiven. Rather, he likely refers to his past achievements and spiritual growth. As great as were any past growth or spiritual successes that Paul experienced, greater things still were ahead.

He said, "I press toward the goal for the prize of the upward call of God in Christ Jesus." The picture is of an athlete so intent on winning a race that as he ran, his body was bent over and his face was straight ahead. Paul was saying that the direction of his life was upward and onward. Nothing excited Paul more than the thought of one day standing before the Lord and being rewarded abundantly. "I just can't get enough," summarized his spiritual appetite.

Do you know Christ more deeply this month than you knew Him last month? Are you stronger spiritually now than you were six months ago? Are you focusing on where you *are* or where you *need to be?* When it comes to spiritual growth, it is actually *commendable* to be dissatisfied.

To Illustrate

John J. Audubon is considered one of the foremost authorities on wildlife. He would often crouch in a swamp for hours, week after week, just to learn one additional fact about a single bird. One summer, in fact, he went daily to the bayous near New Orleans to observe a shy waterfowl. He stood chest deep in the almost stagnant water, hardly breathing, while poisonous snakes and large alligators passed by. Yet when he talked about his work, he was obviously not satisfied that he had learned enough about a particular bird. He always wanted to know more.

When it comes to our spiritual growth, God desires that we always want to learn more about Christ, deepening our knowledge and walk with Him.

To Meditate

Spiritually, where you are now should be a stepping stone, not a stopping point.

To Pray

Ask God to give you two things: discontentment with where you are spiritually and determination to know Him better.

Day 14

Life in heaven is free.
Reward in heaven is
earned.

To Read

> *And behold, I am coming quickly, and My reward*
> *is with Me, to give to every one according to his*
> *work.*
>
> —Revelation 22:12

To Consider

When you die, heaven is not the only thing that God gives you. Other things are in store for you, and God wants to give you a lot of them. They are called rewards, and they are God's way of responding to the way you have lived for Him and served Him.

We cannot earn eternal life. It is given to us as a free gift the moment we trust Christ. Ephesians 2:8–9 clearly tells us, "For by grace you have been saved through faith, and that not of yourselves; it is the gift of God, not of works, lest anyone should boast."

Then we are told, "For we are His workmanship, created in Christ Jesus for good works, which God prepared beforehand that we should walk in them" (vs. 10). When we live for Christ and do good works, God promises reward in heaven. Whereas eternal life in heaven is free, reward in heaven is earned and is based on faithful obedience to the Savior.

John, the man whom God used to write the book of Revelation, spoke of that reward in connection with the second coming of the Savior. Two things ought to excite you as a Christian about that truth.

One is that Jesus Christ Himself is personally doing the rewarding. No greater person could hand out rewards than the Savior who died for you on a cross. His emphasis on "I am coming quickly" means we ought to anticipate Him at any moment, even though He may not return within our lifetime.

Two, His reward is directly connected with our service for Him. He will "give to every one according to his work." No work done for Christ goes unnoticed and no faithfulness goes unrewarded. We do not know from Scripture all the details connected with those rewards, but the emphasis of Scripture is that we *will* be rewarded.

You can see how the distinction between salvation and reward in heaven shows both the love and fairness of God. He is so loving that anyone who wants to can come to Christ and receive His free gift of eternal life. He is also fair, because there will be reward waiting for us in heaven directly related to the way we live for Him now.

To Illustrate

During a celebration in London after the Crimean War, soldiers appeared before Queen Victoria to receive their medals. An officer of the crown assisted her in pinning awards on the soldiers. As she saw one soldier who had gone through much suffering on her behalf, she wanted to reward him personally. As she pinned the award on him, she is reported to have said, "Well done, good and faithful servant."

To Meditate

The work done *for* Christ now brings reward *from* Christ later.

To Pray

Knowing how God delights in rewarding you, ask Him to make you a faithful follower of Christ in four areas: your home, your job, your community, and your church. Ask Him to keep you mindful that any moment could be the moment of His return.

Day 15 | *Set a high standard every day.*

To Read

But as He who called you is holy, you also be holy in all your conduct, because it is written, "Be holy, for I am holy."

—1 Peter 1:15–16

To Consider

Often people do not see their need for Christ because they compare themselves to others. "I'm not as bad as most people I know," or "I don't go to church, but I live a better life than most of those who do." Perhaps you said those same things before you came to Christ. That kind of thinking fails to see that God's standard is perfection. Measured by that standard, we all come short. But when God gave us His free gift of eternal life, He accepted us based upon His Son's merit, not upon our own.

If we're not careful, we can fall back into those patterns of thinking that characterized us as non-Christians. As we consider how well we're doing spiritually, we're tempted to exclaim, "I'm a lot better person than a lot of Christians I know." Although that might be true, other Christians should not be our standard.

God Himself is our standard. God declares, "Be holy, for I am holy." Jesus Christ saved us, and He is coming again. We need every day to fix our eyes upon Him as our standard. We are to live a life completely separated from sin and committed to righteousness. We should strive to be holy as He is holy.

Will we fail to meet His standard of perfection? Daily! When we fail, we need to live in the joy of His forgiveness. But a failure to meet His standard should not prevent us from reaching for it.

Think how your life will be affected by that kind of standard. Do you try to keep your mind as pure as His? Do you consistently respond to others the way He does? Do you love people as deeply as He does?

Having Christ and His holiness as your standard raises the bar on each day. You no longer want to live as well as other Christians live; you want to live as holy as Jesus Christ did.

To Illustrate

When a surgeon selects a scalpel to use in the operating room, he or she chooses one that is clean and purified. A scalpel that has a minute spot is rejected as quickly as one that is severely defiled. The *degree* of defilement is immaterial. The *fact* of defilement is what matters to a good and careful surgeon. As followers of Christ we should be as concerned about purity in our lives as a surgeon is about the purity of his or her instruments.

To Meditate

The holiness of Christ should be not only an example to live by but a standard to reach for.

To Pray

A man once prayed, "Lord, make me as holy as it is possible for a saved sinner to be." Pray that prayer on a consistent basis, knowing that it will encourage a higher level of purity and holiness.

Day 16 | *Leave your old baggage behind.*

To Read

But now you yourselves are to put off all these: anger, wrath, malice, blasphemy, filthy language out of your mouth. Do not lie to one another, since you have put off the old man with his deeds, and have put on the new man who is renewed in knowledge according to the image of Him who created him.

—Colossians 3:8–10

To Consider

Imagine you've been invited to a formal reception. Your flight schedule doesn't allow time to change clothes before the event, so you'll need to go directly from the airport to the reception dressed in your brand-new formal attire. But when you step off the plane wearing your elegant clothing, you carry a small suitcase that has seen better days. The handle is broken, the corners are taped, the scars are deep, and the entire suitcase is discolored. The old baggage doesn't go with the new look.

All of us, when we come to Christ, carry into our new lives some old baggage—sins that used to characterize us. Some examples are listed in Colossians 3: anger, wrath (outbursts of temper), malice (cruelty toward others), blasphemy, filthy language, and lying. It's understandable that these used to characterize us, considering our former master—Satan.

Now, as children of God, we have a new master. God's Holy Spirit lives within us. Just as the "old man" had the image of the old life, the "new man" can now bear the image of Christ.

How do we leave this old baggage behind? By "putting off" the old and "putting on" the new. The Bible calls that obedience. We now take instructions from a different person—Christ. The old baggage needs to be left behind and replaced with whatever honors the Lord. Anger needs to be replaced with forgiveness, and filthy language with a proper use of the tongue.

All the old baggage, however, doesn't disappear overnight. But as we grow as Christians, God makes us increasingly sensitive about which baggage to discard because it doesn't fit the new person we are in Christ. Day by day He helps us to leave that old baggage behind.

To Illustrate

When John Rolfe married Pocahontas and took her to England as his wife, the esteemed Indian princess began a life completely different from the life she had known among her people in America. She left her old life and became the wife of an English gentleman, and she began to acquire the characteristics of her new society. Her new position required of her a new way of living. She had to "put off" the old and "put on" the new.

To Meditate

New Christians still have old baggage, but obedience allows the old to be put off so the new can be put on.

To Pray

As you seek to discard old baggage, ask God to help you be quick to do two things: acknowledge sins that were part of your old life and then, in instant obedience, leave those sins behind.

Day 17

If somebody offends you, talk to that person, not about that person.

To Read

Moreover if your brother sins against you, go and tell him his fault between you and him alone. If he hears you, you have gained your brother.

—Matthew 18:15

To Consider

A sign in the break room of an office complex caught everyone's attention. It said, "Don't talk about yourself. We'll do that after you leave."

Humorous but convicting, isn't it? How many times as non-Christians were we accustomed to talking about people behind their backs? Unfortunately, even Christians can fall into the same habit.

As Christians we are brothers and sisters in Christ. There will be times when, to a small or large degree, we hurt each other. How does God want us to handle those who offend us? He wants us to talk *to* them, not *about* them.

Matthew 18:15 says, "If your brother sins against you. . . . " God doesn't tell us what kind of sin He has in mind, because the nature of the sin is immaterial. A person may malign our character or be irritable and sarcastic in conversation. The person may or may not be aware of the sin he or she has committed. When you approach that person with his or her sin against you, God wants the conversation to be private, not public.

Why? Your ultimate goal is not to rebuke; it is to restore. Your goal is to convince the person in the privacy of your relationship that what he or she did was wrong, so that, recognizing it, the person may apologize and live in the joy of forgiveness. When approached lovingly and directly, many people regret the wrong and apologize. By approaching lovingly and directly, you can gain your sister. Your face-to-face conversation in love can produce a *better* brother rather than a *bitter* brother.

You might ask, what if the person won't admit he or she is wrong? The verses following Matthew 18:15 give a step-by-step procedure to be followed, but start where Scripture starts—talking *to* that person, not *about* that person. Stop and think about it. If *you* hurt someone, would you want that person to talk *to* you and not *about* you? Therefore, in following Christ's command, we are doing unto others as we would have them do unto us.

To Illustrate

William Norris was an American journalist who specialized in simple rhymes that packed a lot of meaning. He once wrote:

> If your lips would keep from slips,
> Five things observe with care:
> To whom you speak; of whom you speak;
> And how, and when, and where.

When we have been offended, God makes the "to whom you speak" and "of whom you speak" very clear. Speak to the one who offended you.

To Meditate

If someone in the body of Christ does something commendable, let the whole world know. If someone does something offensive, tell just that person.

To Pray

Ask God to help you so love people in the family of Christ that when they offend you, you do what is sometimes hard but most rewarding. Talk *to* them, not *about* them. Also ask God to help *you* not to be defensive when you are approached about how you may have wronged others.

Day 18

Be realistic—Christians struggle with sin. Prepare for those struggles.

To Read

> *For the good that I will to do, I do not do; but the evil I will not to do, that I practice. . . . I thank God—through Jesus Christ our Lord! So then, with the mind I myself serve the law of God, but with the flesh the law of sin.*
>
> —Romans 7:19, 25

To Consider

Sometimes life is a real struggle. Living for Christ isn't always easy. But when we see Christ face to face, we will be delighted that we chose to live for Him.

As godly as was the apostle Paul, he didn't hesitate to admit his own struggles. Although a Christian, he still had that sinful nature that encouraged him to do wrong. He admitted that his actions didn't always conform to his wishes. The good he wanted to do, he didn't do. The wrong he desired not to do, he did.

How did he resolve that struggle? The answer was found in his relationship with Christ. Through depending upon the Lord, Paul could do what God wanted him to do, not what his sinful nature urged him to do. Each time he was tempted, he recognized he no longer *had* to sin. As a Christian, he could now choose to do what Christ wanted him to do.

Before becoming a Christian you, too, were under the control of your sinful nature. Now in a relationship with Christ, you can serve the law of God instead of the law of sin. Instead of cursing, you are free to control your tongue rather than let it control you. Instead of seeking revenge when others hurt you, you can now choose to forgive them. When tempted to lie, you have His strength to tell the truth.

But don't be fooled. There *will* be struggles. Expect them and recognize where your victory lies. That puts you in the path of doing what is right rather than doing what is wrong.

To Illustrate

An athlete who came to Christ remarked, "Just about the time I think I have the Christian life and all its problems under control, I blow the whole thing and blow it real big! I am learning that the Christian life is not an unending series of conquests. It's often a real struggle. It's learning to get up after Satan knocks me down, wiping the blood and sweat and tears off my face, and jumping back into the middle of the struggle."

To Meditate

As struggles come, answer the question, "Am I going to respond in the way I did under the domination of my sin nature, or in the way I am free to in my relationship with Christ?"

To Pray

Each time you struggle, ask God to remind you of the Person to whom you are related. Then lean on Him to do what you should do, not what you used to do.

Day 19

You are not the owner, merely the manager, of everything you have.

To Read

Command those who are rich in this present age not to be haughty, nor to trust in uncertain riches but in the living God, who gives us richly all things to enjoy. Let them do good, that they be rich in good works, ready to give, willing to share.
—1 Timothy 6:17–18

To Consider

Think of the things that you presently own. Do you own them or manage them? Have you ever thought about the difference between owning and managing? An owner possesses what he has. A manager oversees what belongs to someone else.

By New Testament standards, having more than one day's provisions in the cupboard makes one rich. By that measure, we're all wealthy. Most of us have not only this week's food in the freezer but next week's as well. When Paul wrote to Timothy he instructed him to remind others that it is God who "gives us richly all things to enjoy." Whether we possess a car, a boat, a house, or cash, they are provided by God. He owns them.

God wants us to manage our resources properly and use them for the advancement of His kingdom, not for self-centered living. He emphasized "ready to give, willing to share." Our foremost thought should be how these riches can benefit *others*, not how can they benefit us.

Could you assist a neighbor with his or her unexpected health bills? Is your church sponsoring a clothing drive for the local homeless shelter and needing your assistance? Whenever and however you assist, you are giving what He owns and you manage.

Is buying a new home wrong? No, as long as you recognize that God is the owner and that you are the manager, and you allow the home to be a blessing in your community. Within your walls, a discouraged neighbor should find encouragement, lonely people should find a friend, and unbelievers may be introduced to the Savior. Does making investments dishonor the Lord? Not at all, as long as you manage those investments in a way that would please Him. After all, your finances are *His*.

To Illustrate

In the book *Your Money: Frustration or Freedom*, Howard L. Dayton tells of Jim Seneff, who came to understand that God is the owner of everything he possesses. He bought a car to replace the one he'd been driving, and a young girl drove into the side of it when it was just two days old. Jim's first reaction was, "Well, God, I don't know why you want a dent in the side of your new car, but you have one!"

To Meditate

Everything you have is on loan. God is the owner. You are the manager.

To Pray

Pray that God will keep you mindful on a daily basis that *everything* you have is from Him. Ask Him to help you manage all that He has given you in a way that honors Him.

Day 20

Mental checkups are important to your spiritual health.

To Read

> *Finally, brethren, whatever things are true, whatever things are noble, whatever things are just, whatever things are pure, whatever things are lovely, whatever things are of good report, if there is any virtue and if there is anything praiseworthy—meditate on these things.*

—Philippians 4:8

To Consider

Any part of your body, if not guarded, could get you into trouble, especially if that part represented a weakness before you came to Christ. Your hands could cause you to steal, your eyes could make you covetous, or your tongue could cause you to lie or gossip.

No part of your body, though, must be more carefully guarded than your mind. What enters your mind comes out through your life. Proverbs 23:7 teaches that as a man thinks in his heart, so he is. Mental check-ups are essential in healthy spiritual growth.

Philippians 4:8 teaches that what you allow inside your mind should meet these standards.

Whatever is true. The mind should not tolerate wrong teaching or false rumors.

Whatever is noble. The mind should only accept what is decent and not slanderous.

Whatever is just. The mind should only entertain what God Himself approves.

Whatever is pure. The mind should dwell on thoughts that will encourage good character and conscience.

Whatever is lovely. The mind should dwell on things that produce unity.

Whatever is of good report. The mind should dwell on what is good and commendable in life.

Paul continued, "If there is any virtue and if there is anything praiseworthy meditate on these things." His point is, the mind should always dwell on what is good and positive, not on what is evil and negative.

If an unworthy thought enters your mind, toss it out and replace it with something good. The way you think impacts the way you live.

To Illustrate

In his book *Developing the Leader Within You,* John Maxwell tells of a man in Hong Kong who walked past a tattoo studio. On display were several samples of available tattoos, including one with the words "Born to Lose." Entering the shop, the man expressed his astonishment: "I can't believe that anyone would want that tattoo." The Asian man tapped his head and responded, "Before tattoo on body, tattoo on mind."

To Meditate

What you dwell upon in your thoughts, you will produce with your life.

To Pray

Ask God to help you visualize your mind as having a door. Whatever knocks that is good and positive, allow in. Keep the door closed to whatever is evil and negative.

Just serve, and God will reveal your spiritual gift.

To Read

> *Having then gifts differing according to the grace that is given to us, let us use them: if prophecy, let us prophesy in proportion to our faith; or ministry, let us use it in our ministering; he who teaches, in teaching; he who exhorts, in exhortation; he who gives, with liberality; he who leads, with diligence; he who shows mercy, with cheerfulness.*
>
> —Romans 12:6–8

To Consider

God's greatest gift to you is eternal life. But God doesn't stop there. The moment He saved you He also gave you one or more spiritual gifts.

Spiritual gifts are particular abilities God gives to Christians so that together we can bring people to Christ and help each other grow spiritually. Christians don't all have the same spiritual gifts, but we all have at least one.

The ones mentioned in this particular passage are

Prophecy—the ability to proclaim what God has already revealed in the Scriptures

Ministry—the ability to serve the needs of fellow believers

Teaching—the ability to explain the Bible to others

Exhortation—the ability to graciously encourage and strengthen fellow believers

Giving—the ability to give extraordinarily of all one has

Leadership—the ability to inspire and lead people toward a particular goal

Mercy—the ability to feel deeply for the hurts of others and help those in need

How do you find your spiritual gift? Remember two *E*s—experience and exposure.

First is experience. In the Scripture quoted above, notice the repetitive phrases "let us use them" and "let us use it." God directs moving objects. You don't have to know what your spiritual gift is in order to be used of the Lord. Go ahead and begin serving. Through involvement in a local church, do whatever you can to serve and God will show you what your spiritual gift is.

Second is exposure. As you serve, the godly men and women who observe you often help by pointing out your particular gift. They may say, "I think you have the gift of mercy. You are so compassionate toward people," or "I think you have the gift of exhortation. You really know how to excite and encourage people."

Once you discover your gift, ask God to help you develop it. Be careful not to compare your ability to somebody else's ability. God doesn't expect you to be the best that *they* can be. He expects you to be the best that *you* can be.

To Illustrate

When asked the question, "What can I do?" Theodore Roosevelt gave the perfect answer: "Do what you can with what you have where you are." In terms of developing and using your spiritual gifts, that's all God expects of you.

To Meditate

Your spiritual gift is God's gift to you. The development and use of it is your gift to Him.

To Pray

Ask God to give you the opportunity to serve Him through your local church. Then as you serve, ask Him to help you better understand your spiritual gift and how He would like you to use it.

Day 22

Your family might think you're a religious fanatic.

To Read

> *Do not think that I came to bring peace on earth. I did not come to bring peace but a sword. For I have come to "set a man against his father, a daughter against her mother, and a daughter-in-law against her mother-in-law"; and "a man's enemies will be those of his own household."*
>
> —Matthew 10:34–36

To Consider

Not everyone is convinced you made the right decision in trusting Christ. Some may even be convinced that you made a mistake. Most hurtful, though, is when criticism comes from those who live behind the same doors that you do.

In Matthew 10, as Christ sent out His disciples, He forewarned them that the message about Him would not "bring peace but a sword." He warned that at times His message would create conflict rather than resolve it.

Why? Because the message about Christ is one on which people must take a stand. John 3:18 states, "He who believes in Him is not condemned; but he who does not believe is condemned already, because he has not believed in the name of the only begotten Son of God." Jesus Christ is the dividing line between people. A person's eternal destiny is determined by what he or she does with Christ.

But where does that division often occur? Christ warned, "And a man's enemies will be those of his own household."

As you are vocal about your relationship with Christ, you may upset some of your family members. Some might be offended at your insistence that they need Christ, convinced they are perfectly fine the way they are. Others will urge you to keep that "religious stuff" to yourself. Others may even avoid you, fearing you'll bring up spiritual things.

Pray that those related to you will see their need to be rightly related to Him. Also, ask God to send someone in addition to you to speak to them. Someone outside the family is often used of the Lord to reaffirm the witness of someone inside the family.

To Illustrate

A woman who came to know Christ became deeply concerned about her brother's salvation. When she approached him, he called her a religious fanatic. In response, she wrote him a loving letter explaining the gospel. In the letter she said, "I have nothing to lose. You already think I'm a religious fanatic. You have everything to gain. If you trust Christ you can know you're going to heaven and experience His presence with you while here on earth." God used that letter to soften his heart and bring him to the Savior.

To Meditate

The One who is viewed as dividing earthly families is the One who longs to make our relatives part of His heavenly family.

To Pray

Think of three family members whom you would like to see come to Christ. Ask God to provide (1) an open door for your *own* witness and (2) someone outside the family as an *additional* witness.

Day 23

Specialize in self-examination, not cross-examination.

To Read

> *Judge not, that you be not judged. For with what judgment you judge, you will be judged; and with the measure you use, it will be measured back to you. And why do you look at the speck in your brother's eye, but do not consider the plank in your own eye? Or how can you say to your brother, "Let me remove the speck from your eye"; and look, a plank is in your own eye? Hypocrite! First remove the plank from your own eye, and then you will see clearly to remove the speck from your brother's eye.*
>
> —Matthew 7:1–5

To Consider

It's easy to be critical, isn't it? A person cuts in front of us on the highway and we exclaim, "Does he think he owns the road?" If a fellow employee receives a promotion we ask, "How did she pull that off?" Our critical spirit can lead us to be judgmental.

God wants us as Christians to first examine ourselves, not others.

The above passage gives two cautions. The first one is, don't be too hasty in judging fellow believers. If we are strict, God will likewise be strict in His judgment of us. He alerts us, "With the same measure you use, it will be measured back to you." We as Christians will one day be examined before the Lord to receive whatever reward He deems appropriate. If we want Him to be lenient with us, we need to be lenient with others.

The second caution is, look inward not outward. A plank of wood is a lot larger than a speck. The Lord cautions, before looking at the problems in others' lives we ought to first look at the bigger problems in our own lives.

Many believers note that, upon close examination, what they found irritating in others was often present in their own lives. One believer testified, "I wish I had learned earlier that what I'm most sensitive about in others is something I'm usually guilty of myself."

The world says cross-examine. Christ says self-examine.

To Illustrate

A man was having difficulty communicating with his wife, and he concluded that she was becoming hard of hearing. Without telling her, he decided to put her to the test. With her back to him he sat in a chair on the far side of the room and whispered "Can you hear me?" Receiving no response he moved closer then asked, "Can you hear me now?" It took four such moves until finally he was right behind her. When he asked, "Can you hear me?" she responded with frustration, "For the fourth time, yes!"

To Meditate

If you are merciful in your examination of others now, God will be merciful in His examination of you later when you stand before Him to be rewarded.

To Pray

Jesus Christ was known for being gracious and merciful. Ask God to make you the same way in your interactions with others. Always ask, "Where do I need to change?" before asking, "Where do they need to change?"

Day 24

Love is not an emotion. It's an act of the will.

To Read

> *A new commandment I give to you, that you love one another; as I have loved you, that you also love one another. By this all will know that you are My disciples, if you have love for one another.*
>
> —John 13:34–35

To Consider

In the early days of Christianity, when non-Christians viewed a group of believers, they often made the observation, "How they love one another!"

Love. That's what Christ wants to see in Christians—maturing disciples who are characterized by love. Christ said, "By this all will know that you are My disciples, if you have love for one another" (John 13:35). But what is love? Love often becomes confused with lust and is reduced to nothing more than emotion.

Two things characterize the love that we are to have for each other. First, a biblical definition of love is putting the other person first, even if it means sacrificing yourself. Christ set the standard when he said "as I have loved you." He took our sins upon Himself and suffered the punishment we should have suffered. Superior to anything that anyone had ever known, such love was a new commandment.

Second, love is not an emotion. It's a choice. Christ explained, "A new *commandment* I give to you, that you love one another." Love springs from an act of the will as we choose to obey Christ. He calls on us to follow in His steps and do as He has done. Feelings or emotion may or may not be present. We may feel that a particular person is not worthy of our love. Regardless, we are asked to make a conscious choice that says, "I will love you. I will put you first even if it means sacrificing myself."

To Illustrate

Some explorers were trapped in the frozen tundra near the South Pole. Progress was slow, and it was doubtful that the team would make it back to their base. The food supply had dwindled to only a few biscuits in each person's knapsack. One night as they were sleeping the leader heard a movement. With eyes barely open, he watched a member of the team reach toward another's knapsack. The leader was shocked, thinking the man had stooped so low as to become a thief. Then he saw the man take half a biscuit out of his own bag and place it very quietly in the other's. That generous team member had observed his companion growing weak and thought that the other might be too proud to accept someone else's rations. That night the team leader witnessed a demonstration of sacrificial love.

To Meditate

Loving others is not a just feeling to be followed but, most importantly, a commandment to be obeyed.

To Pray

Ask God to help you obey His command to love others regardless of your desire or feelings. Then measure your love by His standard, not yours.

Day 25

Be quick to call sin what God calls it—sin.

To Read

> *If we confess our sins, He is faithful and just to forgive us our sins and to cleanse us from all unrighteousness.*
>
> —1 John 1:9

To Consider

We cannot fully grasp how God feels about sin. Because God is a holy God, sin is repulsive to Him. The most repulsive act to us does not come close to how repulsive sin is to God. That's why when we disobey, He wants us to call it what He calls it—*sin*.

Do not misunderstand a tremendous truth of Scripture. Once you have trusted Christ, your relationship with God can never be broken. You are His forever. Your *closeness* to the Lord, though, can be impacted because of sin. In the above passage, John was speaking to believers: "If we confess our sins. . . ." To *confess* means that when we do wrong God wants us to agree with Him about what He calls it—*sin*.

Don't soften or downplay sin. God doesn't. Call a lie *a lie*—not a mistake. Call adultery *adultery*—not an affair. Call sin what God calls it.

What happens when we confess our sin? God is faithful and just. He is true to Himself. Being a loving and compassionate God, He will be quick to "forgive us our sins and to cleanse us from all unrighteousness." He is able to do so because when His Son died on a cross two thousand years ago, He took the punishment we deserved for *all* sins, past, present, and future. Once we confess sin, we can live with the comfort that what we have done is forgiven. Since the sin is not on God's mind, it no longer needs to be on ours.

Think of a parent/child relationship. When the child misbehaves, the relationship is still the same. The parent is still the parent and the child is still the child. But if the child does not deal with his or her error, the child's closeness to the parent will be affected. Once the child confesses the wrong, it is as though it never happened. Similarly, when we call sin what God calls it, our closeness with God is restored, and we know we are completely clean before God. Then, in sincere sorrow and regret, we can take the appropriate actions in dealing with the consequences of our sin. How much better to walk before God in the excitement of forgiveness instead of in the agony of unconfessed sin.

To Illustrate

A woman approached a well-known evangelist after one of his messages and asked, "Can you help me? I have a terrible habit of exaggeration." "Certainly, madam," replied the evangelist. "Just call it lying."

To Meditate

When sin is understood for what it is, confession can be painful, but the forgiveness is exhilarating.

To Pray

Is there sin in your life that you have not dealt with before God? If so, confess it to Him and ask Him to forgive you. Pray, too, that He will give you a consistent quickness to admit sins to Him so that you can live in the joy of His forgiveness.

Day 26

The Christian life has low moments!

To Read

For indeed, when we came to Macedonia, our bodies had no rest, but we were troubled on every side. Outside were conflicts, inside were fears. Nevertheless God, who comforts the downcast, comforted us by the coming of Titus, and not only by his coming, but also by the consolation with which he was comforted in you, when he told us of your earnest desire, your mourning, your zeal for me, so that I rejoiced even more.

—2 Corinthians 7:5–7

To Consider

A Bulgarian proverb states, "God promises a safe landing but not a calm passage." Not only does the Christian life lack calmness, it sometimes has low moments. Paul the apostle experienced them, and so will we. Don't be surprised when they come.

Paul said, "our bodies had no rest" because tension and strain affected him both mentally and physically. He didn't mention specific troubles, but "outside were conflicts" probably refers to conflicts he experienced with unbelievers as he preached the gospel. Some people were receptive to his message and others weren't. By "inside were fears" he probably refers to his concern for the new converts. He had written a letter to the Corinthian church, confronting them about some unacceptable behavior, and he was uncertain how the letter had been received. He also may have been fearful that Satan would try to trip up the believers in some sin.

God has ways of comforting us when we are down, and this time He used Paul's good friend Titus. Titus explained to Paul how the attitude of the Corinthians had changed. They had a great desire to see Paul again and were mourning for their past behavior. Paul was thrilled to see his friend Titus, but even more thrilled when he heard his report.

The Christian life is not sorrow-free. Our down moments have different causes—loss of a job, health problems, unexpected bills, tension in the family, a big hurdle erected in front of our plans. There *will* be low moments, but God's comfort, regardless of how it comes, will be sufficient for those moments.

To Illustrate

Tom Landry, long-time coach for the Dallas Cowboys, was a committed Christian whose order of priorities were (1) God, (2) family, and (3) football.

What separated him from many other coaches was his vision and ability to put devastating setbacks behind him. He once testified in *USA Today,* "I suffer after losses, but fortunately do recover quickly. My relationship with Christ gives me a source of power I would not have otherwise." As Christians, we too suffer disappointments and setbacks, but Christ provides the power in the midst of them.

To Meditate

The Savior promises that we'll have no low moments in heaven, but we'll have low moments on earth. Don't be caught off guard when they come.

To Pray

Ask God to help you live consistently for Him, during both the up moments and the down ones.

Day 27 | *Temporary suffering can result in eternal reward.*

To Read

> *In this you greatly rejoice, though now for a little while, if need be, you have been grieved by various trials, that the genuineness of your faith, being much more precious than gold that perishes, though it is tested by fire, may be found to praise, honor, and glory at the revelation of Jesus Christ.*
>
> —1 Peter 1:6–7

To Consider

Low moments, as we observed yesterday, are not unusual in the Christian life. Sometimes those moments are particularly hard. Suffering comes from different directions and in varying amounts.

In the passage above, Peter was writing to both Jews and Gentiles who were living outside their native homeland in present day Turkey. Persecution had likely caused them to scatter. In A.D. 62, the Roman emperor Nero heightened his persecution of believers, and physical suffering became severe.

Some Christians were thrown before wild beasts, and others were burned as torches to give light at night. Christians feared for their lives and escaped to other countries.

Most of us will not face severe persecution. But there is not a Christian alive who sooner or later won't endure trials. All of us, sometime between now and when we see the Lord face to face, will be "grieved by various trials . . . for a little while." Those trials can result from circumstances beyond our control. Peter encourages us, reminding us of the temporary nature of trials, but admits they will be the cause of grief.

How should we respond? Rejoice not *because* of trials but in the *midst of* them. Why? Because of their outcome. Peter continues, "The genuineness of your faith, being much more precious than gold that perishes, though it is tested by fire, may be found to praise, honor, and glory at the revelation of Jesus Christ."

This verse describes a goldsmith who put gold in a crucible, subjected it to intense heat, and liquefied the mass. The impurities rose to the surface to be skimmed away, so that when the metal worker saw his reflection in the surface of the liquid, he knew that the remaining contents were pure gold. Similarly, as our faith is tested by trials and we respond properly, our faith is worthy of praise, honor, and glory at the appearing of Christ. There will be eternal reward when we see Christ face to face.

To Illustrate

A woman who endured much suffering asked her pastor, "When am I going to get out of all these troubles?" He wisely answered, "You should have asked, '*What* am I going to get out of all these troubles?'"

To Meditate

Suffering is expected and temporary. When we respond properly, reward is promised and is eternal.

To Pray

Thank God now for the hard moments you have already faced. Confess any wrong attitudes as being sin and ask Him to forgive you. Then ask for His help in responding to all hardships in a proper and biblical way.

Day 28

Since you are part of another world, don't love this one.

To Read

> *Do not love the world or the things in the world. If anyone loves the world, the love of the Father is not in him. For all that is in the world—the lust of the flesh, the lust of the eyes, and the pride of life—is not of the Father but is of the world. And the world is passing away, and the lust of it; but he who does the will of God abides forever.*
>
> —1 John 2:15–17

To Consider

The moment you came to Christ, your home address changed! The Bible tells us, "For our citizenship is in heaven, from which we also eagerly wait for the Savior, the Lord Jesus Christ" (Philippians 3:20). In relation to this world, remember that we are just passing through.

Since this world is not our future home, we should

not emotionally attach ourselves to it. That's what God had in mind when He said, "Do not love the world or the things in the world." *Love* has the idea of cherishing something. We ought not cherish the world and its contents.

Examine the common sense behind God's exhortation: "If anyone loves the world, the love of the Father is not in him." This caution doesn't mean that someone who loves the world is not a Christian. It simply means that the person is not letting the love of God be a controlling influence in his or her life.

Why does God want us to not love the world? Because the nature of the world will only harm us spiritually, not help us. The "lust of the flesh" refers to the sinful desires that drive us to sins such as immorality. The "lust of the eyes" refers to those things that Satan sets before us and that cause cravings that are detrimental to our walk with Christ, making us covetous and materialistic. The "pride of life" is a pride of who we are and what we have in this present world.

All things that are part of this world are passing away. Money and notoriety don't last forever. As Christians we are part of the permanent, not the passing. We ought to cherish what abides forever— close fellowship with God.

Enjoy everything that God gives you, and use it in a way that honors Him. But don't cherish the world. The next world—not this one—is your home.

To Illustrate

A German emigrant and his family heard so many tales about America they felt like they knew the country well. The emigrant so loved the land he had not yet seen that as he departed for America, his mother said, "You are going home, and I am staying in a foreign land."

To Meditate

Citizens of heaven should cherish the place where they will abide for eternity, not the place where they are living temporarily.

To Pray

Ask God to help you make Him the source of your affection and to help you not become attached to worldly attractions that are detrimental to your spiritual growth.

*Don't lose your contact
with non-Christians
—but be careful!*

To Read

> *Now it happened, as Jesus sat at the table in the
> house, that behold, many tax collectors and sin-
> ners came and sat down with Him and His dis-
> ciples. And when the Pharisees saw it, they said to
> His disciples, "Why does your Teacher eat with
> tax collectors and sinners?" When Jesus heard that,
> He said to them, "Those who are well have no
> need of a physician, but those who are sick."*
>
> —Matthew 9:10–12

To Consider

Someone who cares for you probably played a part
in your coming to Christ. God wants you to be what
Jesus Christ was—a friend to sinners—and spend
time with non-Christians that they, too, might come
to the Savior.

The above text refers to "many tax collectors and

sinners." Tax collectors were despised because they over-taxed the people and kept the remainder for themselves. Sinners were despised because of their lack of moral purity and their degenerate lifestyle.

The religious faction known as the Pharisees, therefore, found it inappropriate for a "teacher" of God's Word to eat with those whom the Pharisees felt were a filthy class of people. Christ's explanation was simple—those who are well do not need a physician, but those who are sick do. Tax collectors and sinners often came to Christ because they felt their need of Him. The Pharisees needed Him, too, but their spiritual pride kept them from admitting their sin.

God wants you as a new Christian to spend time with believers so that you can encourage one another, but don't leave your non-Christian friends behind. Spend time with them that they might come to know Him.

One word of caution! If you find yourself slipping spiritually when you are around unbelievers, do what is appropriate to keep that from happening. Remember, Jesus Christ influenced the sinners. They did not influence Him.

To Illustrate

Bobby Richardson was a believer who was deeply burdened for his friend and baseball teammate Mickey Mantle. Mickey played hard and partied even harder. Mickey never seemed to see his need for Christ until June 1995, when doctors informed him that cancer had destroyed his liver. He then realized that he was staring death in the face. Not only did Mickey ask Bobby to pray for him but Mickey's family asked Bobby to come visit him. When Bobby walked into Mickey's hospital room and went over to the bed, Mickey told Bobby what he had been waiting to hear. Mickey said, "Bobby, I've been wanting to tell you that I have trusted Jesus Christ as my Savior." Tears came to Bobby's eyes as he realized that the man who had been his friend for life would now be his friend for eternity.

To Meditate

In your relationships with non-Christians, God wants you to be their friend so you can introduce them to your Friend.

To Pray

Ask God for two kinds of relationships—a close relationship with believers who can stimulate you spiritually, and contact with non-Christians whom you can introduce to the Savior.

Day 30

When you explain the gospel, explain it clearly.

To Read

For by grace you have been saved through faith, and that not of yourselves; it is the gift of God, not of works, lest anyone should boast.

—Ephesians 2:8–9

To Consider

Ask your friends, "What do you have to do to get to heaven?" They will usually mention going to church, living a good life, keeping the commandments, taking the sacraments, or being baptized. If this is how they respond, they have missed the message that eternal life is free. So when you speak to others about Christ it is absolutely critical that you present the gospel *clearly*.

Grace means favor we do not deserve. As sinners, we do not deserve God's kindness. We deserve to be separated from Him forever in what the Bible calls hell. But God extends to us favor we do not deserve. He punished His perfect Son, Jesus Christ, when

He should have punished us. Christ died as our *substitute*. When He arose the third day He proved to everyone that He had conquered sin and the grave.

How then are we saved? As Paul reminded the Ephesians, "For by grace you have been saved through faith." *Faith* means to trust or depend upon. As sinners who deserve to be forever separated from God, we must recognize that Jesus Christ died in our place and rose again, and place our trust in Christ alone as our only way to heaven. As the verse explains, "It is the gift of God, not of works, lest anyone should boast."

If we could get to heaven through something we did, we could brag, "I did it!" But God did everything in providing for our salvation, and it is a gift from Him. Therefore, our "bragging" has to be in what Christ did on the cross, not in what we have done.

So when you speak to your friends about their need of Christ, explain that (1) we are sinners, (2) Christ died for us and rose again, and (3) eternal life is a free gift that comes through trusting Christ alone to save us. To be of eternal help to your friends when presenting the gospel, be sure to present it clearly.

To Illustrate

John Newton wrote "Amazing Grace," a song that is sung at both religious and secular events. As he became elderly, he began losing his memory. On one occasion he said, "My memory is nearly gone but I remember two things—that I am a great sinner and that Christ is a great Savior." The clear message all our friends need to hear is the *simple* message that we are great sinners, but Christ is a great Savior. Only through trust in Christ can we receive His free gift of eternal life.

To Meditate

Presenting the gospel clearly helps people see sin at its worst and the love of God at its best.

To Pray

Ask God to help you consistently look for opportunities to share the gospel. Pray that when He gives those opportunities, He will help you present the gospel clearly.

Day 31

Salvation is the starting point, not the stopping point.

To Read

> But grow in the grace and knowledge of our Lord
> and Savior Jesus Christ. To Him be the glory both
> now and forever.
>
> —2 Peter 3:18

To Consider

You have come to know the only One who can give the free gift of eternal life. God, though, doesn't just want you to merely *be* a Christian. He wants you to *grow* as a Christian. That's right! Salvation ought to be the starting point, not the stopping point.

Grow in the above verse carries the idea to "be continually growing." Growth ought to be a never-ending process. You should never be at a spiritual standstill. What direction should your growth take? Peter says, "Grow in the grace and knowledge of our Lord and Savior Jesus Christ." *Grace*, as we noted yesterday, means favor we do not deserve. *Knowledge* means a better understanding of who Christ is. God wants us to know better the undeserved kindnesses that He has extended to us, and wants us to deepen our understanding of who Christ is. Like in human relationships, as you learn and grow, you will better know your newfound Savior one month from now than you do today. In fact, growing as a Christian will keep you from being led astray from the truth of God's Word. You will move forward spiritually rather than backward in the Christian life.

How do you grow? You've just finished this thirty-one day devotional. Now read the book of Philippians, one of the easiest books of the New Testament, finishing just one chapter each day, looking for one truth to meditate on the entire day. Philippians has four chapters, so on the fifth day start over again with chapter one. Stay in that book for a month. You'll discover things during the second read through that you didn't see in the first, and you'll discover things in the fourth read through that you didn't see in the third. Upon concluding your study of Philippians, keep moving through the entire New Testament, covering a chapter a day, a book of the Bible each month. As you prayerfully apply what you have learned, you will never stop growing spiritually. Your life will be characterized by spiritual freshness, not spiritual stagnancy.

To Illustrate

In his book *The Fisherman and His Friends,* Louis Albert Banks tells of a man who came upon a pine tree blown down by a severe storm near the shores of Lake Superior. Examining it closely, he discovered it to be 250 years old. One thing, though, impressed him most as he stripped away the bark. It was evident that on the day the tree fell, it was still growing! May you so learn and so grow that even on the day your earthly life ends, you are still growing.

To Meditate

One of the greatest needs of a Christian is the need to know Christ better.

To Pray

Thank God for the thirty-one truths you have learned through this devotional. Ask Him to use your own personal Bible study to help you learn one truth each day that will impact the way you live from this day forward.

31 Days with the Master Fisherman

A Daily Devotional on Bringing Christ to Others
by R. Larry Moyer

Since many things are better caught than taught, this book encourages readers to spend time in reflection and meditation on the subjects of discipleship and evangelism. As we spend time considering the things closest to Jesus' heart, we will catch His vision for sharing the Good News.

This one-month daily devotional book is designed to encourage all believers to join in the Great Commission to share the Good News and to improve each person's skills in the greatest fishing expedition of all time!

0-8254-3178-6 / 96 pp.

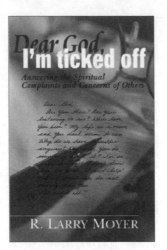

Dear God, I'm Ticked Off
Answering the Spiritual Complaints and Concerns of Others
by R. Larry Moyer

This book answers many of the questions most commonly asked by non-Christians. Moyer examines the mind-set and thinking of the questioners while exploring the issues they raise, such as

- If God is so great, why are His people so awful?
- If God is as loving as the Bible claims He is, how can He send anyone to hell?
- How can I trust the Bible when it was written over 2000 years ago?
- Why would a happy person need Jesus?

0-8254-3175-1 / 144 pp.

Also available from Kregel Publications

Free and Clear
*Understanding and Communicating God's Offer
of Eternal Life*
by R. Larry Moyer

This handbook will lead believers step-by-step into a
thorough understanding of the gospel message's
terminology and concepts. Group discussion questions
are included at the end of each chapter.

"This book is for any pastor or layperson who takes the
Great Commission seriously. . . . I think you'll come away
with a fresh appreciation for the salvation we have in Christ,
and a renewed desire to present the gospel to others."
—Luis Palau

0-8254-3177-8 / 272 pp.

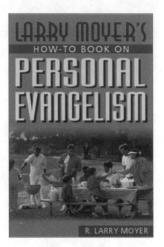

**Larry Moyer's How-To Book on
Personal Evangelism**
by R. Larry Moyer

"I can't share the gospel. I'm afraid I'll say something wrong—that is, if I knew what to say to begin with!" Have you ever found yourself thinking this? Larry Moyer draws from his twenty-five years of experience in evangelism as he introduces readers to the exciting reality that believers *can* learn how to share the gospel with others—confidently.

Even if you think evangelism isn't for you, this step-by-step resource shows you how to start and nurture an evangelistic lifestyle.

0-8254-3179-4 / 128 pp.

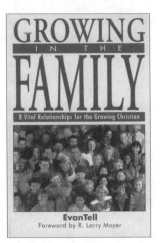

Growing in the Family

8 Vital Relationships for the Growing Christian
by EvanTell Resources; Foreword by R. Larry Moyer

Being a part of God's family means more than simply attending a church service each Sunday. It means growing in our understanding of God's will for our lives and growing in our relationships with God and others.

Growing in the Family is a practical, easy-to-follow guide designed to help new believers dig into the Bible and discover basic truths for themselves. While this study is helpful for the individual reader, it is designed for use in discipleship training classes and small group Bible studies, as well.

0-8254-3173-5 / 144 pp.

EvanTell, Inc. is an association committed to a clear presentation of the gospel through a careful study of the Scripture. Its three main activities are:

CONFERENCES TO REACH

Operation Friendship is a church outreach featuring a Saturday night outreach dinner and a Sunday morning outreach service, both directed toward non-Christians. A mini-seminar for believers follows on Sunday evening, addressing how to overcome major struggles in evangelism.

SEMINARS TO TEACH

The popular *You Can Tell It!* seminar, taught by an approved instructor, helps believers overcome their two greatest struggles in evangelism—fear of rejection and not knowing how to present the gospel.

The *You Can Preach It!* seminar gives thorough and practical instruction in developing biblical, evangelistic messages relevant to non-Christians.

MATERIALS TO EQUIP

Books, booklets, cassettes, videos, and an extensive training program prepare and strengthen believers for their ministry of evangelism.

PO Box 741417
Dallas, Texas 75374-1417
1-800-947-7359